美国公民

How We Organize Ourselves | Non-Fiction Series

Copyright © 2022 by Level Learning, INC. and Washington Yu Ying PCS™
Original and Edited Text Copyright © 2022 by Washington Yu Ying PCS™

All rights reserved. No part of this book in whole or part may be reproduced without written permission from the publisher.

Published by Level Learning, INC.

Content Contributors:
Washington Yu Ying PCS™ - Feng Dong, Pearl Zao He You
Level Learning - Jingyao Qi

Illustrations by: Josh Taira

Leveling classification based on Level Learning standard.
For full description, visit www.levellearning.com

ISBN 978-1-64040-119-8
Simplified Chinese Edition

About Level Learning:
Level Learning provides a literacy focused curriculum specifically designed for K-12 Chinese as a Second Language classrooms. Our program offers 20 levels of specific and detailed objectives, leveled texts and passages, mastery-based online assessment, and analytics to enable data-driven instruction. Level Learning reading curriculum for both literature and informational text emphasize grammar and comprehension skills to help teachers develop confident and independent Chinese language readers. The non-fiction series of books are specifically designed to support our informational text course based on multiple national standards. To learn more about our entire offering, visit www.levellearning.com.

About Washington Yu Ying PCS™:
Washington Yu Ying PCS is a Mandarin English dual language immersion International Baccalaureate (IB) World school. Yu Ying's mission is to inspire and prepare young people to create a better world by challenging them to reach their full potential in a nurturing Chinese/English educational environment. Yu Ying's comprehensive IB, dual immersion curriculum equips students with global competencies for success in the real world. As a leader in immersion education, Yu Ying is determined to advance Chinese language programs and global citizenry education by helping other schools create and strengthen their Chinese programs. For more information, email: products@washingtonyuying.org

什么是公民？拥有一个国家国籍的人，就是这个国家的公民。美国公民就是拥有美国国籍的人。

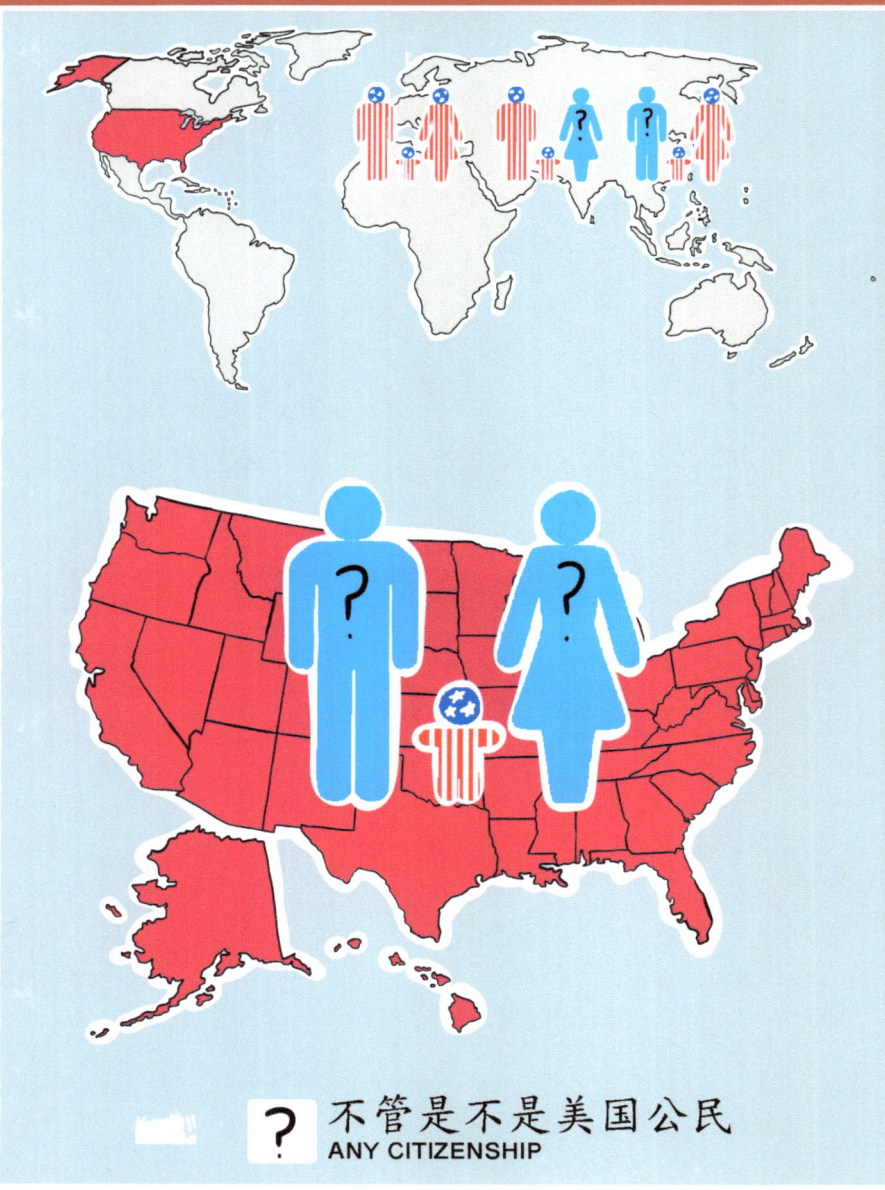

一般来说，不管父母是不是美国公民，只要是出生在美国的人，就是美国公民。有的孩子没有在美国出生，但是父母双方或者一方是美国公民，那这个孩子也是美国公民。

UNITED STATES OF AMERICA — PERMANENT RESIDENT

Surname

Given Name

USCIS#   Category

Country of Birth

Date of Birth   Sex

Card Expires:
Resident Since:

长期在美国居住的人不一定就是美国公民。这些人可能是从别的国家来到美国的。在美国工作或者和美国公民结婚，可以让这些人拿到美国绿卡（永久居民卡）。拥有绿卡不代表他们是美国公民。但是他们可以在美国合法居住。

如果拥有绿卡的人想成为美国公民,他们需要向移民局申请,然后接受面试。申请人需要知道最基本的美国政治和历史知识。

双重国籍就是一个人拥有两个国家的国籍。有些国家不接受双重国籍。如果一个人申请成为美国公民，他可能需要放弃原来的国籍。

公民有权利也有义务。美国公民有选举权和被选举权。美国公民也享有一些福利，比如奖学金、医疗补助等。美国公民也有义务，比如陪审等。

你是在哪里出生的？你是哪个国家的公民呢？

Glossary

	Pinyin	English Definition
公民	gōng mín	citizen
拥有	yōng yǒu	to have
国籍	guó jí	nationality
一般	yì bān	general
结婚	jié hūn	to get married
绿卡	lǜ kǎ	green card
永久居民卡	yǒng jiǔ jū mín kǎ	Permanent Resident card
代表	dài biǎo	to represent
合法	hé fǎ	legal, lawful
移民局	yí mín jú	immigration office
申请	shēn qǐng	to apply
面试	miàn shì	to interview
基本	jī běn	basic
政治	zhèng zhì	political
历史	lì shǐ	history

	Pinyin	English Definition
知识	zhī shi	knowledge
双重	shuāng chóng	dual
放弃	fàng qì	to give up
选举权	xuǎn jǔ quán	the right to vote
被选举权	bèi xuǎn jǔ quán	elected
享有	xiǎng yǒu	to enjoy
福利	fú lì	welfare
奖学金	jiǎng xué jīn	scholarship
医疗补助	yī liáo bǔ zhù	medical insurance
义务	yì wù	obligation
陪审	péi shěn	jury duty

www.ingramcontent.com/pod-product-compliance
Lightning Source LLC
Chambersburg PA
CBHW041226070526
44584CB00001B/115